Warring According to Prophecy

Warring According to Prophecy

Terry Crist

Warring According To Prophecy

Terry Crist Ministries
P.O. Box 35889
Tulsa, OK 74153

ISBN: 0-88368-225-7
Printed in the United States of America
© Copyright 1989 by Terry Crist

Unless otherwise indicated, all Scripture quotations are taken from the *King James Version* of the Bible.

Whitaker House
580 Pittsburgh Street
Springdale, PA 15144

Dedication

I dedicate this book to my two sons, Terry Michael III (Mickey) and Joshua Levi, whose lives are a testimony to the principles upon which this book has been written.

What a great privilege and responsibility it is to raise two little warriors who are already an important part of this last-day prophetic revival. (Acts. 2:17,18.)

Contents

Introduction

As we enter the 1990s, I believe a sense of destiny will overcome the Body of Christ. This is the hour in which end-time saints and ministries will see the fulfillment of all things that have been prophesied since the world began. (Acts. 3:21.) I am convinced that, as far as the Church is concerned, the 1990s will come to be known as the decade of destiny.

The destiny of the Church of Jesus Christ will be fully revealed in this hour. The eternal purpose of God will be made manifest before every living creature — whether fleshly, heavenly or demonic. (Eph. 3:9-11.)

It is time that we Christians begin to realize that the Church has not been set in the earth just to occupy space. We are not here to sit on comfortable pews, listen to motivating sermons and do nothing to affect the nature and destiny of our world. We are not here to gain a natural reputation for ourselves or to impress the world with our sanctity or prosperity. We are here to make an impact upon society through the power of the Gospel and to bring about a change in the hearts of men. *There is a vast difference between impressing society and making an impact upon it. Impressions are easily forgotten, while impacts leave lasting results.*

We in the Church must realize that we are aliens on a mission. God has set us here for a divine purpose, and that purpose must be fulfilled through the life of every believer.

God has a planned destiny for the life of each one of us, as well as for the Church as a corporate body. The Church has been in the mind of God since before the foundation of the world was laid. (Eph. 3:11.) The Church is not an "after thought." It is not the result of some hastily-conceived backup plan that was put into effect 2,000 years ago to save God from embarrassment because His primary plan had failed. God has always had an eternal destiny in mind for the Church as a whole and also for each of our individual lives.

Very few believers have a true sense of destiny for their lives. Most spend their entire existence in a state of perpetual wonderment. They pass their whole lives wondering what their purpose is or what is their calling in the Kingdom of God. As a pastor, I see far too many Christians who are wandering aimlessly through life with no purpose or direction. They lack fire and zeal.

Oh yes, they are "bound for heaven," because they have been born again. Their difficulty is not in preparing for heaven, it is in dealing with this earth. They are perpetually in a tranquil state of mediocre existence. Few believers ever dare to step past the line of mediocrity and "press toward the mark for the prize of their high calling in Christ Jesus." (Phil. 3:14.)

Once you catch a glimpse of your destiny in God, your life will never be the same. A vision of destiny will change every aspect of your life. It will alter the way you walk, talk, live and breathe. You will become a person of destiny.

People of destiny carry about them a purposeful air. They walk tall and speak boldly. They are confident, forceful men and women. They know and understand their mission in life. They have purposed in their hearts to make the necessary sacrifices and to accept the essential responsibilities of bringing about God's plan. People of destiny refuse to settle for anything less than God's perfect will in their lives.

Such people know that they are not living in this day and hour as a result of coincidence, but that God has strategically placed them in this particular time and place. Isaiah 41:4 declares that God is the One Who calls the generations from the beginning. That means that He orchestrates the generations. In the beginning of time, He determined to place *you* in this particular generation to serve as an end-time saint and minister.

People of destiny cannot be sidetracked. They may sometimes be enticed with false promises, but they will never allow that enticement to become a substitute for their divine purpose in life. If they happen to get off track, they are quick to repent, make the necessary adjustments and get back on course.

When a vision of destiny comes alive within you, you will not be content with anything less than the fulfillment of that vision. Material things will not fulfill you. Houses, automobiles, properties and bank accounts will not satisfy your deepest longings. Nothing will fill the void within except walking in the steps that God has chartered for your life.

It is to assist you to discover that divine destiny and to walk in those God-ordained steps that I have written this book.

Terry Crist

1
The Return of the Prophet

As we progress in the '90s, prophetic ministries will begin to stir us up concerning the God-ordained destiny for our lives. They will begin to give us understanding regarding the eternal purpose of God for the Church.

At present there is much confusion in the Body of Christ concerning the ministry of the prophet and the operation of simple prophecy. Don't become alarmed by the confusion that abounds. Any time true revelation knowledge begins to come forth, the powers of confusion, error and deception rise up to attack it so the people cannot flow strongly in it.

This is the day and the hour in which the prophets of God are beginning to come forth in the land. The ministry of the prophet is returning to the earth in full force!

Prophetic Restoration

And it shall come to pass afterward, that I will pour out my spirit upon all flesh; and your sons and your daughters shall prophesy, your old men shall dream dreams, your young men shall see visions:

And also upon the servants and upon the handmaids in those days will I pour out my spirit.

Joel 2:28,29

As I travel throughout the nations, I am beginning to see a fresh emphasis being placed on the necessity of prophetic ministry. There is an awakened desire for the voice of the Lord to be trumpeted loud and clear throughout the land.

In this present wave of prophetic restoration, we will see a great diversity of prophetic ministries arise. There will be young prophets, old prophets, prophets to certain groups of people, singing prophets, preaching prophets, praying prophets, teaching prophets, weeping prophets, governmental prophets, prophets to specific churches and nations. Each of these prophets will have a distinctive ministry and anointing. They will also have a different ranking and authority within the realm of their ministry gift.

Prophetic Responsibility

Along with this prophetic restoration, there is a divine responsibility being placed upon the prophets to assume their rightful position of authority in the Spirit. God will demand great accountability from prophetic ministries in this hour, as well as from the other fivefold ministry gifts. As the prophets of God begin to take their place in the land, we will begin to see the prophetic word of the Lord flowing like mighty rushing waters from Zion. God is raising up end-time ministries which will be extremely developed at delivering the word of the Lord boldly and accurately.

Warning Signals

In the midst of this awakened hunger for prophetic ministry there are many dangers which we must be aware of. I have often seen great harm done to the Body of Christ because of "soulish" manipulation and the operation of demonic control under the guise of prophetic utterances.

Some devastated believers have even opted to throw out the practice of prophetic ministry after receiving one too many false prophecies and "bean dreams." They have become weary of being the victims of fleshly and demonic manipulation. They have been seriously hurt, both emotionally and spiritually.

As a result of this devastation, some have developed a distrust and a despising of prophetic utterances. They have become frightened of this vital ministry of the Holy Spirit, and have erected "walls" and "barriers" to guard against further hurt. Sadly enough, the devil's counterfeit has brought great reproach to the genuine ministry of the prophet and the operation of simple prophecy.

If this hurt and fear is not resisted, it will quench the manifestation of the Holy Spirit. The Apostle Paul emphatically warned the Thessalonians:

> **Quench not the Spirit.**
>
> **Despise not prophesyings.**
> **1 Thessalonians 5:19,20**

The Body of Christ has missed many visitations of God because of fear and a lack of true spiritual discernment. A lack of discernment will prevent you from receiving the benefits of true prophecy.

All too often, sincere Christians allow their hunger for the manifestations of the Holy Spirit to override their discernment.

If your desire for the supernatural is greater than your discernment, then you are a prime candidate for deception.

2

The Nature of Prophecy

There are many things that we must understand regarding prophetic utterances. One of the most important is the fact that *prophecy is conditional*. When you begin to look through the Word of God, you will discover that everything God spoke to His people through the prophets was dependent upon certain conditions.

Have you ever received a prophetic word which bore witness with your spirit — and yet you waited in vain for that word to be manifested in your life? Even though you believed the word and waited patiently for it to come to pass, it remained unfulfilled.

Prophecy is conditional. If you don't recognize that truth, then you will never receive the fulfillment of your prophecy.

In giving a prophecy to His people, God always says, "If you will, I will." Unless you understand this principle, you won't be able to judge prophecy correctly, according to the Spirit and the Word of God. Many times prophets are labeled as false prophets simply because the conditions of their prophecy were never fulfilled.

The Prophecy of Jonah

As an illustration, let's look at the story of Jonah. It provides us a perfect example of conditional prophecy.

You remember that Jonah was a prophet, although a reluctant one. He was called by God to deliver a prophetic message to the city of Nineveh; yet he ran from his divine calling. As a result, God said to him, in essence, "Jonah, I'm going to get you. You can run but you can't hide."

Let's begin our study by examining Jonah's divine commission:

> **Now the word of the Lord came unto Jonah the son of Amittai, saying,**
>
> **Arise, go to Nineveh, that great city, and cry against it; for their wickedness is come up before me.**
>
> **Jonah 1:1,2**

But notice Jonah's response to God's call upon his life:

> **But Jonah rose up to flee unto Tarshish from the presence of the Lord, and went down to Joppa; and he found a ship going to Tarshish: so he paid the fare thereof, and went down into it, to go with them unto Tarshish from the presence of the Lord.**
>
> **Jonah 1:3**

Jonah's reaction to God's command was: "No, I don't believe I will go to Nineveh. I have a much nicer plan for my life." So he boarded a vessel bound for Tarshish in a futile effort to "flee from the presence of the Lord." We all remember what happened next: how a storm arose, how the sailors sought the person responsible, how the lot fell on Jonah who confessed his sin against God, how he was thrown overboard and swallowed by "a great fish" which God had prepared for that purpose. (Jonah 1:4-17.)

But we also recall that after three days and three nights in the belly of the fish, Jonah repented and was vomitted out on dry land. (Jonah 2:1-10.)

> **And the word of the Lord came unto Jonah the second time, saying,**
>
> **Arise, go unto Nineveh, that great city, and preach unto it the preaching that I bid thee.**
>
> **So Jonah arose, and went unto Nineveh, according to the word of the Lord. Now Nineveh was an exceeding great city of three days' journey.**
>
> **And Jonah began to enter into the city a day's journey, and he cried, and said, Yet forty days, and Nineveh shall be overthrown.**
>
> **Jonah 3:1-4**

Notice very carefully that when Jonah finally complied with God's command and went to Nineveh where He began to prophesy against the city, he did *not* give the people who heard his message an opportunity to repent. He did not come to them preaching a message of hope. He did not even give the residents of Nineveh room for their faith to operate. He simply proclaimed that in forty days the city would be destroyed.

> **So the people of Nineveh believed God, and proclaimed a fast, and put on sackcloth, from the greatest of them even to the least of them.**
>
> **Jonah 3:5**

As a result of Jonah's preaching, the people of that great city actually believed God and went into fasting and mourning, crying out to the Lord in genuine repentance.

> **And God saw their works, that they turned from their evil way; and God repented of the evil, that he had said that he would do unto them, and he did it not.**
>
> **Jonah 3:10**

In this instance, God changed His mind. He turned from His original plan and declared that He would not do to the people of Nineveh what He had decreed in the beginning.

Prophecy Is Conditional

Now I would like for us to look at this situation from Jonah's perspective. He has been out on the streets prophesying that God is going to totally destroy the city of Nineveh. Now suddenly God tells him, "No, Jonah, I've changed My mind; I'm not going to destroy Nineveh after all."

So how does this make Jonah appear in the natural? It makes him look like a false prophet. (You see, the people of Nineveh don't know about the private conversations between God and Jonah, so they don't know *why* Jonah's prophecy is not fulfilled!)

> **But it displeased Jonah exceedingly, and he was very angry.**
>
> **Jonah 4:1**

So Jonah became "displeased." And why not? After all, his reputation as a prophet of the Lord was on the line. *He was more concerned about personal validation than he was about the salvation of the city of Nineveh.* He was more interested in how he looked in the eyes of the people than he was in seeing them repent and be spared from God's wrath and judgment.

So what does he do? He takes his grievance to the Lord:

> **And he prayed unto the Lord, and said, I pray thee, O Lord, was not this my saying, when I was yet in my country? Therefore I fled before unto Tarshish: for I knew that thou art a gracious God, and merciful, slow to anger, and of great kindness, and repentest thee of the evil.**
>
> **Therefore now, O Lord, take, I beseech thee, my life from me; for it is better for me to die than to live.**
>
> **Jonah 4:2,3**

Jonah was "washed up." He felt that his ministry was over. He was so distraught and displeased he wanted to die.

If you and I had lived in Nineveh during those days, we might have called Jonah a false prophet. He wasn't, however; his prophecy was simply conditional.

The Prophecy of Isaiah

What about the time Isaiah came in and prophesied to King Hezekiah?

> **In those days was Hezekiah sick unto death. And the prophet Isaiah the son of Amoz came to him, and said unto him, Thus saith the Lord, Set thine house in order; for thou shalt die, and not live.**
>
> **2 Kings 20:1**

After Isaiah had delivered his message and left, the king turned his face to the wall and began to pray, asking God to spare his life. As a result, the heart of God was moved to alternative action:

21

And it came to pass, afore Isaiah was gone out into the middle court, that the word of the Lord came to him, saying,

Turn again, and tell Hezekiah the captain of my people, Thus saith the Lord, the God of David, thy father, I have heard thy prayer, I have seen thy tears: behold, I will heal thee: and on the third day thou shalt go up unto the house of the Lord.

And I will add unto thy days fifteen years....

2 Kings 20:4-6

Although his first prophecy to the king did not come to pass as he had said it would, Isaiah was not a false prophet either. Like that of Jonah, his prophecy was simply conditional.

The fulfillment of prophetic utterances is predicated upon conditions. So when we hear prophetic utterances come forth, we must understand that many times our response will determine the fulfillment of the prophecy.

3

Prophecy and the Laying On of Hands

This charge I commit unto thee, son Timothy, according to the prophecies which went before on thee, that thou by them mightest war a good warfare.

1 Timothy 1:18

In this passage, Paul is referring to another time when Timothy had received prophecy. In another place in this same epistle we see that there was a time and season when Timothy was set apart for the work of the ministry. The presbytery laid hands on him. Evidently Paul had prophesied to him regarding his ministry calling:

Neglect not the gift that is in thee, which was given thee by prophecy, with the laying on of the hands of the presbytery.

1 Timothy 4:14

Two Ways of Conveying Spiritual Gifts

Now there were two ways that the gifts were conveyed to Timothy. First, his gifts were spoken into him. Paul stood under the inspiration of the Holy Spirit and spoke the prophetic word that went into Timothy and created within him a spiritual deposit.

You see, when a prophet brings forth a prophecy by the Spirit of God, he can speak things into other people that will create a spiritual deposit within them.

While Paul was speaking under the inspiration of the Holy Spirit, his words loosed a spiritual gift which entered into young Timothy.

Second, Timothy's gifts were placed in him by the laying on of hands:

Wherefore I put thee in remembrance that thou stir up the gift of God, which is in thee by the putting on of my hands.

2 Timothy 1:6

So Timothy had the gifts which had been deposited in him by the Spirit of God. They were resident within him and were established in his life. The devil couldn't steal them, because God had placed them there. You see, the gifts and callings of God are without repentance (Rom. 11:29.) They are forever deposited in the life of the person to whom they are given. Yet it was up to Timothy to take those gifts and begin to put them into operation.

Activating Spiritual Gifts

And from the days of John the Baptist until now the kingdom of heaven suffereth violence, and the violent take it by force.

Matthew 11:12

Spiritual gifts may have been placed in you, whether by prophecy, by the laying on of hands or by the sovereign work of the Holy Spirit. But unless you learn how to take those gifts and forcefully put them into operation, you can live your whole life and never see them bring forth fruit in you.

There are many people all over the world who have gifts of God in them, but their gifts are not flowing or operating. These gifts are not manifesting themselves because the people who possess them do not know how to resist the devil and put their gifts into action.

It is sad to realize that there are prophets of God who are cleaning tables at restaurants or pumping gas in service stations. They have nowhere to preach, no place to minister. They wander aimlessly without any sense of purpose or destiny. They are in bondage because they don't know that their gift needs to be taken by force and brought forth and established in the earth. They are not aware that they must "war a good warfare." (1 Tim. 1:18.)

If you have a spiritual gift, it was placed in you in order for you to "war a good warfare" and to fulfill the will of God for your life. Your gift wasn't placed in you to help you make money. It wasn't deposited there to assure you material success. Its purpose is not to bring you fame or fortune or to cause you to be lifted up in praise and adulation. The gift was placed in you to equip you to do a work of God in the earth.

You can live your entire life and never see that gift come forth. If that happens, it doesn't mean that the gift wasn't there. It simply means that you never knew how to take hold of that gift and begin to war with it and to cause it to come forth so it could fulfill the purpose God gave it to you to accomplish.

I've met people all over the world who are getting up into the latter years of their lives and are just beginning to discover their spiritual gift. They have been born again for years, but are only now finding their calling.

Oh, don't be one of those people. Don't wait until the end of your life to discover your gift. Locate it now. Work with it now. Let it manifest itself now. Don't wait. The Church needs your gift now. The lost need it now. Not tomorrow. Not next year. Today.

Warring with the Prophecies

So spiritual gifts had been deposited in Timothy by prophecy and by the laying on of hands. These gifts had been placed there by divine deposit. Then Paul instructed Timothy to war with the prophecies, to use them as tools to establish the will of God in his life.

When someone prophesies the word of the Lord to you, along with that word there always comes a great responsibility. Nothing in the Kingdom of God is ever established by casual living. Spiritual gifts come by grace, but it takes power to establish them in your personal life and to cause them to become vital, working and operative.

Until you take that word and war with it, it will be of no use to you or anyone else. You must say to the adversary: "Devil, loose my destiny. I break your influence over my future; let it go. I choose to believe the word of God." Unless you learn to exercise authority in that manner, the devil will thwart your purpose in God. Too many precious Christians have received the word of the Lord and yet allowed Satan to come in and stop it from coming forth in their lives, because they did not know how to war according to prophecy.

You may still have those prophecies which were given to you written down in the cover of your Bible, yet they are not working in your life. The reason is because you have allowed the enemy to come in and blind your eyes and deaden your ears. You have let Satan thwart God's plan for your life.

Timothy had to war with his prophecies. He had to fight. He was called; he was anointed; the gift had been placed in him; he had been given exciting glimpses of the plan of God for his life; but when it came down to "the bottom line," he had to war to see those gifts put into operation and God's divine purpose manifested in his personal life.

So must you and I.

4

Operating Prophecy by Faith

Prophecy always requires two things: 1) faith, and 2) obedience.

Shortly after the passages described in Chapter 3, Paul told Timothy to:

Fight the good fight of faith....

1 Timothy 6:12

...according to the prophecies which went before on thee, that thou by them mightest war a good warfare;

Holding faith....

1 Timothy 1:18,19

Holding faith is an aggressive action!

In order to see your prophecy fulfilled, you must fight with faith, aggressively. You must hold fast to faith. If God has promised you something, then He is faithful and just to fulfill that which He has spoken. But in order to bring forth that prophecy in your life, you have to hold faith. You've got to "fight the good fight of faith."

Faith is a spiritual force which will bring forth the manifestation of God's *rhema* (His spoken Word) in the life of the person who receives it. God will speak a word; that's a manifestation of grace. Yet faith must take hold of that word and establish it in the personal life of the individual to whom that word is given.

Faith causes the word to function. That word must become practicum in your life, and not just theory. Unless your faith is operating to take hold of God's plan and purpose for your life, His word will not manifest itself.

No Faith, No Profit

Let us therefore fear, lest, a promise being left us of entering into his rest, any of you should seem to come short of it.

For unto us was the gospel preached, as well as unto them: but the word preached did not profit them, not being mixed with faith in them that heard it.

Hebrews 4:1,2

In this verse we see that the word of God was preached to this particular group of people, but it did not profit them. The word was straight out of the inspiration of the Holy Spirit, but there was no profit to those who heard it. Why? Because that word was not mixed with faith.

When there is no faith, there is no profit. Without faith, there are no results. Faith will bring about results. It will turn situations around because it is a weapon of spiritual warfare. In fact, faith is the basis for operating all of our spiritual weapons.

Faith Is a Fight

For whatsoever is born of God overcometh the world: and this is the victory that overcometh the world, even our *faith*.

1 John 5:4

The whole arena of faith is a realm of conflict. Faith is "the victory that overcometh the world."

Faith is something that you use as a weapon to defeat the powers of darkness and to bring forth the fullness of God into your life. When doubt and unbelief begin to assail you and you start to feel that the promise of God will never manifest itself, that is the time to begin to wage war with your faith. That's when you must declare boldly and in power: "I know the word of the Lord will come to pass. God is faithful. That which He has spoken will be performed. Heaven and earth will pass away, but God's word will never fail."

The Voice of Faith

God has told me to cross this country and stir up the prophetic words which have been deposited in the Body of Christ. As I preach and teach, I am seeing former prophecies begin to come alive in the minds and hearts of God's people. If God has given you a personal word of prophecy, don't let it go. Let it grow.

If God has promised you something, that promise will be fulfilled — if you don't let go of that word which has been deposited in you. It will come to pass, if you won't get discouraged because it hasn't happened within your time frame. If you have waited three weeks, then wait three more! Then at the end of that time, if the word still hasn't been manifested, then wait three more weeks! Don't give up. Don't let go. Keep fighting. When you get out of bed in the morning, take that prophetic word and begin to war with it. Let the devil know that you've not forgotten it, but that it is alive within you.

Faith has a voice; it has a bold utterance in the Spirit. Faith is never silent!

You must take that word of prophecy and begin to stir it back to life within you. Let the voice of faith declare your purpose: "God has said that my ministry will be fulfilled in the earth! God has said that my business will prosper! It was prophesied to me. I heard it with my own ears. My spirit bore witness to it, and now I will see it fulfilled. Satan, let go of my prophecy. You have no right to rob me of my divine calling and purpose."

Begin to declare it. Repeat it over and over. Say it until it becomes established in your life. In order to do what God has called you to do, you must be bold. Some people want to whisper what God has said to them. If you are afraid that someone may hear you, then you are never going to see your prophecy manifested. If you don't have the faith to shout out boldly what your purpose is, then you probably don't have the faith to bring it to pass.

A person who is full of doubt and unbelief is usually real good about waiting until things come to pass before speaking. Once the word of God has been manifested for all to see, then he will say, "Bless God, I knew it was going to happen all the time."

However, faith will speak out what is going to happen before it takes place. And what is spoken will come to pass. If you have a word from God, then you must be bold.

Jesus Our Example

Let's look at how Jesus operated in faith when He was only a twelve-year-old boy. Even at that early age

He constantly confessed the revealed will of God for His life.

> **And when he was twelve years old, they went up to Jerusalem after the custom of the feast.**
>
> **And when they had fulfilled the days, as they returned, the child Jesus tarried behind in Jerusalem; and Joseph and his mother knew not of it....**
>
> **And it came to pass, that after three days they found him in the temple, sitting in the midst of the doctors, both hearing them, and asking them questions.**
>
> **And all that heard him were astonished at his understanding and answers.**
>
> **Luke 2:42,43,46,47**

So here Jesus is in the midst of the temple debating with the doctors of the law, asking them questions and answering their questions. When His parents come to Him, they are amazed and ask Him, **...Son, why hast thou thus dealt with us?...**(Luke 2:48). His answer to them is: **...How is it that ye sought me? wist ye not that I must be about my Father's business?** (Luke 2:49).

From the time He was a child, Jesus boldly declared what His mission in life was. He boldly declared what the will of God was for His life, and it didn't matter to Him if it disturbed people, even His own earthly parents. It certainly didn't bother Him that it stirred up religious devils.

Release the Utterance!

You see, when you begin to speak out the word of the Lord, it will stir up religious opposition against you too. Jesus constantly spoke out of His spirit His mission in life, and what God had called Him to do in the earth. (Luke 4:16-30.) The religious leaders of His day were angry at the forthrightness with which He declared His Father's will. Yet Jesus kept on speaking forth His mission and calling.

Do you know what happens when words like that go forth? They release power. *Your bold anointed utterance (confession) is a weapon of war!* Part of warring according to prophecy is releasing the utterance of God out of your mouth, boldly declaring what God has called you to do and to be.

5

Releasing the *Rhema* of God

And take the helmet of salvation, and the sword of the Spirit, which is the word of God.

Ephesians 6:17

The sword of the Spirit is God's word, His *rhema*. It is God's personal word for you today. It is God's utterance into your life for the situation you are in right now.

This sword of the Spirit is not a dead, dry book. Some people go to meetings and when they are told to war in the Spirit, they hold up their Bibles and wave them. That is not what warring in the Spirit is all about. You can meet the devil face to face and shake the Bible at him all day long and it won't intimidate him one bit. I'll tell you what puts the devil to flight; it's the amount of the word of God which has been deposited on the inside of you, the amount of God's word which has become revelation knowledge working in your life.

So when this verse speaks of the sword of the Spirit, it is referring to God's *rhema*, His word for the moment. It is God's personal thought, His feelings and ideas on a particular subject, at a precise moment in time, spoken to a specific person.

Prayer: the Activating Force

Praying always with all prayer and supplication in the Spirit....

Ephesians 6:18

Now let me point out something about this verse. The actual weapon is not prayer; it's the *rhema*. You may ask, "What about the emphasis that God is now placing on spiritual warfare and intercession?" These are both valid means of attacking the enemy's strongholds, but the actual weapon involved is the *rhema*.

Prayer is the activating force that takes the word of God — the *rhema* — and causes it to be effective. That's why many times people will war in the Spirit and not see results. It's because they are not warring with the word of God. They are just playing soldiers; parading around in military apparel. They are warring with no revelation knowledge of God's plans and purposes. And that kind of warring is ineffective.

Without an understanding of God's plan and purpose, you will wear yourself out warring and never achieve anything. But if you will discover the *rhema* of God and begin to war with it, you'll supernaturally begin to experience breakthroughs.

The word of God is the weapon. Prayer is the driving force behind the word.

Paul said,: "I am not as one who fights ineffectively. I don't beat the air." (1 Cor. 9:26.) Paul had a purpose in mind when he did battle. He knew who he was warring against and what he was fighting for. He also knew the word of the Lord on the subject at hand.

Prayer takes the *rhema* and pushes it through to accomplish its purpose. When someone speaks a prophetic word into your life, and you take prayer in the Spirit and begin to war with that prophetic word, you are pushing that word through to the accomplishment of God's goal and purpose:

> **So shall my word be that goeth forth out of my mouth: it shall not return unto me void, but** *it shall accomplish that which I please,* **and it shall prosper in the thing whereto I sent it.**
>
> **Isaiah 55:11**

Warring with the *Rhema*

We begin to war with the *rhema* of God by praying it forth in the Spirit. And that kind of spiritual warfare is effective.

In Luke 1:37, we read that **...with God nothing shall be impossible.** The original language paints a much clearer word picture. It actually reads something like this: "...no utterance *(rhema)* of God is without power." *God's word has its own power to accomplish its own purposes. However, to benefit from that power you must tap into it and put it to work on your behalf.*

6

Walking in Faith and Obedience

As we stated earlier, the fulfillment of prophecy is dependent upon two factors: 1) faith, and 2) obedience in the Spirit.

The Body of Christ has much to learn about the proper way to respond to prophetic utterances.

Obedience is the secret to bringing God's word to fulfillment.

When a prophecy is given, whether to an individual or a corporate assembly, it demands immediate obedience. If God says, "It's time to repent," then He means for us to repent *now!* If He says, "Rejoice, My people, rejoice," then He means for us to begin rejoicing *now!*

Too many times the Body of Christ has placed very little value on heeding the voice of God. When God speaks, often we don't respond until it is convenient for our flesh to do so. We have not learned to respond immediately in obedience. And that kind of laxity on our part is grievous to the Holy Spirit. It will quench the utterances of God.

The Holy Spirit becomes grieved when people don't respond to His will in His timing! Many times I have seen a prophetic utterance come forth in a church service, but by the time people got around to responding to it, the anointing had lifted. We must become immediate in our response to the voice of God.

Obedience Requires the Proper Response

Another thing which grieves the Spirit and hinders His moving is an improper response to His revealed word.

For example, some time ago I was in a national convention in which God spoke prophetically and said: "The hour has come for My people to begin to cry aloud once again in intercession. The intercessors must come out of the closets where they've been hiding, and return to their position in the Spirit."

At the conclusion of the prophecy, people began to react exuberantly. They shouted and whistled and clapped. They didn't know how to respond correctly to what what God was saying.

Instead of applauding, they should have been praying! The grace had just been released to them to begin to intercede in the Spirit, and they had gone off on a tangent. If God says to pray, He doesn't mean for us to clap! If He says to repent, He doesn't intend for us to rejoice! We must respond to the heart of God as He desires for us to respond, not as we desire.

When the people in that meeting began to shout and applaud, immediately the Holy Spirit became grieved, and the anointing departed from the meeting.

If we expect to reap the benefits of prophecy, we must respond to it properly by the Spirit of God.

7

Judging Prophetic Utterances

As an end-time saint and minister, one of the most vital qualities you can develop is the ability to discern between truth and error. We are quickly entering into an age in which "new revelations" are springing forth everywhere throughout the land. Tragically, most of these "new revelations" are not really new — and they are not really revelations. They are simply a fresh emphasis placed upon age-old deceptions.

In the coming days, spiritual discernment will be an absolute necessity for the protection of your walk with the Lord. We are living in a time in which the powers of darkness are attempting to prevent the Body of Christ from walking in truth. It is also very dangerous to go here and there seeking after a prophetic word. As with any spiritual manifestation, *if your desire for the supernatural is greater than your power of discernment, then you are a prime candidate for deception.*

I believe that the Church of the 90s will be confronted with a deluge of false teaching. In this crucial hour, every truth that we hold dear will be challenged. I see the greatest challenge in this day as coming from diverse elements within the religious community rather than from the general society. The Apostle Paul stated that in the end times **...evil men and seducers shall wax worse and worse, deceiving, and being deceived** (2 Tim. 3:13). He also stated:

> **Now the Spirit speaketh expressly (openly, visibly), that in the latter times some shall depart from the faith, giving heed to seducing spirits, and doctrines of devils;**
>
> **Speaking lies in hypocrisy; having their conscience seared with a hot iron.**
>
> **1 Timothy 4:1,2**

Notice very carefully, Paul did not say that these people would depart from religion. He didn't even say that they would depart from the local church. He said that they would depart from *the faith*. This phrase, "the faith," does not refer to faith for miracles — faith to heal the sick, raise the dead, or show forth signs and wonders. It refers to the basic *Christian faith*, the foundational tenets of God's written Word — the principles of sound doctrine.

I want us to carefully consider the word *depart* in this passage. It is the English translation of the Greek word *aphestemi*, meaning "(to) desert." It calls to mind the image of a soldier in battle who abandons his assigned mission in order to take advantage of a better offer from the other side.

Some of the greatest deceivers of Paul's day were members of religious circles. They were skilled orators and teachers who had no love for the truth. These men were "deserters" — those who forsook "the faith" in order to satisfy their own fleshly desires. Today we might call them "mercenaries" — men who don't care which side they fight on as long as the price is right.

> **For there are many unruly and vain talkers and deceivers, specially they of the circumcision:**

Whose mouths must be stopped, who subvert whole houses, teaching things which they ought not, for filthy lucre's sake.

Titus 1:10,11

If such deceivers had already infiltrated the New Testament Church within fifty years of the ascension of our Lord Jesus Christ, imagine what condition the Church must be in today almost two thousand years later! The time has come when we can no longer allow ourselves to rely on someone else's revelation of the Word of God. We must obtain revelation knowledge for ourselves, and then be willing to "hold fast that which is good." (1 Thess. 5:21.)

Immature Prophets Vs. False Prophets

Quench not the Spirit.

Despise not prophesyings.

Prove all things; hold fast that which is good.

1 Thessalonians 5:19-21

As born-again believers, each of us has a precious ability to hear and know the voice of the Holy Spirit in our lives. (1 John 2:20,21,27.) Along with this ability, every believer possesses the God-given right to judge prophetic utterances. This is not a license to despise or attack those who are babes in prophetic ministry. It is a safeguard to protect us from false prophets whose hearts are not after God.

There is a great difference between an immature prophet and a false prophet. Many times an immature prophet will make mistakes (sometimes severe ones) on the road to maturity, but he will always be willing to repent of his error and repair the damage that he may have caused. However, a false prophet isn't concerned about the damage he has caused to the people of God; his desire is to profit from them. And he does so by the use of seduction and deception.

The fundamental difference between an immature prophet and a false prophet is the condition of his heart. I am convinced that many false prophets have been overlooked as being simply immature, while many immature prophets have been labeled "false," thus destroying their lives and ministries.

A prophet is not false simply because of the inaccuracy of some of his prophecies or because of a lack of spiritual discernment. An individual can be sincere, devout and anointed, yet still be immature and inexperienced in the realm of prophecy. He may be overzealous, which causes him to misunderstand or misinterpret what God is truly saying. Delivering a few inaccurate prophecies does *not* make an individual a false prophet. I have yet to meet any prophet who is infallible. In fact, all of the five-fold ministry gifts are fallible because they are housed in and exercised by mortal beings. Because we are *flesh*, we are subject to mistakes.

If a teacher makes a mistake in his Hebrew/Greek or in his types and shadows, most people are quick to understand. If an Evangelist places a Bible character in a wrong setting during one of his messages, most people would forgive him. If a Pastor gives wrong counsel regarding an individual's finances, most people would swallow hard and forgive him. Yet when a prophet misses it, most people are ready to burn him at the stake!

Jesus Christ is the only human being who ever lived without making a mistake. He possesses the only infallible ministry. As long as we Christians live in unglorified flesh, our ministries will be fallible. It is very possible for a true prophet to be inaccurate occasionally. He will never be purposely so, for a true prophet would rather not speak at all than to misdirect anyone.

A false prophet, on the other hand, has no such scruples. He is a false prophet not because he makes mistakes but because he is first of all a false person. He lives a false lifestyle of deception and purposeful error. He always looks out for his own benefit and welfare and not for the best interests of others.

Test the Spirits

Beloved, believe not every spirit, but try the spirits whether they are of God: because many false prophets are gone out into the world.

1 John 4:1

I want you to notice very carefully that the context of this passage is not dealing with spiritual warfare, or even with deliverance. Here the Apostle John is writing in direct opposition to the false prophets who were creating havoc and confusion in the early Church.

The basis by which any ministry should be judged is the spirit out of which it operates. Correct doctrine is not enough for sound ministry. Right doctrine and a wrong spirit will ultimately bring about a corruption of that which is good. I would far rather associate myself with those who have a right spirit even though their doctrines may not be fully correct, than to associate with those who have correct doctrine and a rotten spirit. If your heart is right, ultimately your wrong ideas of doctrine will be corrected, but a wrong heart will corrupt any right doctrine which you may have.

I have often observed that a wrong spirit always precedes the introduction of the "doctrines of devils." (1 Tim. 4:1.)

> **Now the Spirit speaketh expressly, that in the latter times, some shall depart from the faith, giving heed to seducing spirits and doctrines of devils.**
>
> **1 Timothy 4:1**

Seducing spirits always precede doctrines of devils in manifestation. When an individual gives his ear to entertain seducing spirits, he will eventually end up believing and propagating corrupt doctrine.

When seducing spirits are operating in an attempt to lead a person astray, they often "pull" on the self-life of the soul. People often become seduced by trusting in their physical senses (appetites of the flesh) rather than in the Word of God.

When a minister refuses to judge himself according to the Word of God, he opens the door for wrong spirits to enter and begin to manifest. When demonic spirits and ungodly attitudes are in manifestation in his life, deception begins to be released upon the ears of those who sit under his ministry. It is impossible to be exposed to deceptive voices for very long without being affected in a detrimental way.

How to Test the Spirits of Prophets

In 1 John 4:1, we are told to "try (test) the spirits." I would like to share several questions we should ask in order to test the spirits of those who prophesy to us, and thus identify the false prophets who have come among us:

1. Is the message these people deliver supported by the Scriptures?

In an hour when a fresh emphasis is being placed on the gifts of the Spirit and prophetic utterances, we must clearly recognize the written, established Word of God as the highest spiritual authority. When any spoken revelation does not align itself with the precepts of God's Word, it is obviously inspired by a demonic source.

In this age, there is a strong pull to subtly draw the Body of Christ away from the basic fundamentals of the established *Logos*. If we allow ourselves to give anything else preeminence in our lives, we open the door to false teachers, prophets, and doctrines.

2. Does their ministry bear fruit?

Now this is the area in which many believers are led astray by false prophets and teachers. They equate *fruit* with signs, wonders, and miracles instead of with a godly *manner of living*. They are constantly running from one meeting to the next in an attempt to keep up with the latest revelation. And when miracles are claimed to be occurring, they are willing to swallow the latest fad in revelations.

Signs, wonders, and miracles are not adequate fruit of ministry. In fact, as we enter further into the closing of this age, we will see that lying signs and wonders will become quite common. (2 Thess. 2:9; Rev. 13:13,14.) Jesus warned us of what would occur in the last days when He addressed the disciples in the Sermon on the Mount:

> **Beware of false prophets, which come to you in sheep's clothing, but inwardly they are ravening wolves.**
>
> **Ye shall know them by their fruits. Do men gather grapes of thorns, or figs of thistles?**
>
> **Not every one that saith unto me, Lord, Lord, shall enter into the kingdom of heaven; but he that doeth the will of my Father which is in heaven.**
>
> **Many will say to me in that day, Lord, Lord, have we not prophesied in thy name? and in thy name have cast out devils? and in thy name done many wonderful works?**
>
> **And then will I profess unto them, I never knew you: depart from me, ye that work iniquity.**
>
> **Matthew 7:15,16,21-23**

3. Does their lifestyle glorify God?

Another means of testing the spirits of the prophets is by testing the prophets themselves. Often people feel that the messenger is unimportant; this is a great falsehood. The lifestyle of the messenger is of utmost importance in determining the validity of the message. As I have already mentioned, it is quite impossible to receive a pure word if it has been filtered through a vessel of unrighteousness.

The Holy Spirit is beginning to emphasize the necessity of accountability among ministries in the Body of Christ. No longer can men isolate themselves from the rest of the Body without standing in a place of great danger. Many times extreme individualism and isolation in a ministry is a sign that deep problems exist. Accountability among ministers produces safety.

We must fully know the manner of lifestyle of those who labor among us. This knowledge does not usually come overnight; it comes by observation of the fruit of a long-term relationship with God. The Apostle Paul consistently encouraged the New Testament Church to examine his lifestyle. (1 Thess. 1:5; 5:12; Heb. 13:7.) He became completely transparent before the people so the Lord Jesus Christ could be glorified through him. (2 Tim. 3:10; Eph. 6:21.)

How to Respond to a False Prophecy

If you have been the object of a fleshly or demonic-inspired prophecy, don't sit passively by, hoping that it won't have any lasting spiritual effect upon you.

Words are powerful vehicles in the realm of the spirit. They are containers that carry one source of power or another. Proverbs 18:21 declares that the power of life and death are resident in the tongue. When a false prophecy is spoken over you, it releases powers of death upon you — death to your true calling, ministry gift, anointing, and possibly even your physical body! The power of a false prophecy must be broken in the spirit realm. It must be prevented from coming to pass.

If you are a victim of such a prophecy, begin to war against it. Use your supernatural weapons of the Holy Spirit and resist those false words. (2 Cor. 10:3-5.) Combat them with the power of the blood, the name of Jesus, bold intercession, and prophetic declarations.

Stand up boldly and proclaim: "The plan of the devil will not be accomplished in my life! In the name of Jesus I break the power of false words spoken over me and my family. I will not submit my life and ministry to any false prophecy."

Then begin to declare and decree the true plan of God for your life. The power of truth is always greater than the power of a false utterance.

8

The Power of Prophecy

Everything I am writing about in the pages of this book has been put into practice in my own personal life. Now I would like to share with you a personal testimony of the effectiveness of warring according to prophecy.

Between August 1983 and August 1985, my wife Judith and I went through a season when the power of God's word was tested in our lives. During that period, Judith had four miscarriages, one right after the other, in rapid succession. It was an extremely traumatic time.

Overcoming Despondency and Discouragement

In the early part of 1983 we had been given a prophetic word that we were going to have a child and that he would be a prophet to the nations. At that time we didn't know how to deal with words of prophecy. We thought that if God said something would happen, then it would automatically come to pass. We didn't understand that the person who receives that word has a responsibility to take it and fight with it so that it becomes manifest.

So, one right after another, Judith experienced four tragic miscarriages. Many times people see the effects of such a tragedy on the wife, but I can assure you that it is just as devastating to the husband. The sheer feeling of helplessness was overwhelming! Every time Judith would miscarry, the despondency would hit. Our hopes would go down the drain. We would pull ourselves up by our bootstraps, and then once again the devil would hit us squarely between the eyes.

Immediately after the third miscarriage, Judith was taken to the hospital where she was given a blood transfusion. The blood had not been properly tested and was bad. As a result, she was later diagnosed as "Kell positive." "Kell" is from the erythroblastosis blood-cell group. In layman's terms, it refers to an extreme RH factor. The effect of the "Kell" was the destruction of the white corpuscles in Judith's body which broke down her immunity system. Because of the lack of resistance in her body, she was left susceptible to every type of sickness and disease known to man.

Those who were around us during those days can bear witness to the fact that Judith would contract every sickness that came along. It seemed that if the flu struck the town next to ours, she would catch it. Her body was under constant attack by illness, disease, weakness and infirmity. She was extremely anemic and had no physical strength at all.

Not only was her immunity system weakened, but her chances of ever carrying a child to full term were reduced to almost zero. And all of this came on top of the already existing problems. One doctor told us that if she did become pregnant again, the "Kell" would cross over into the womb and kill the unborn child, or else cause it to be severely deformed.

Crying Out to the Lord

At this time we didn't know how to war in the Spirit. We didn't know about warring according to prophecy. All we knew to do was to cry out to God. If you know nothing in your Christian life except how to cry out to the Lord, that is enough to get you started on the right path so God can release to you more keys of information to set you free: **...whosoever shall call on the name of the Lord shall be delivered...**(Joel 2:32). That means that whoever calls upon the Lord will be healed and freed from bondage.

The knowledge and wisdom of God will be released to you when you begin to call upon the name of the Lord. Judith and I spent hours crying out to God. It was during this time period that God began to give us an understanding of spiritual warfare. So we began to war in the Spirit, to fight against the powers of death and destruction.

Soon we learned that Judith had become pregnant for the fourth time.

Each time Judith lost a child, the miscarriage came at the very same stage of pregnancy (within the 9-12 week stage, though she did carry one child almost six months).

Shortly after the beginning of her fourth pregnancy, while we were out of the country ministering, the same thing began to happen all over again. The attack came right in the middle of a series of meetings we were holding and Judith suddenly became physically ill. Once again she miscarried.

I would like for you to get a picture of what we were up against. Imagine our despair and discouragement. At times we felt like giving up and quitting. The situation seemed hopeless.

End of Rope, Beginning of Hope

But even in those trying times, deep within us there was a flickering of hope that refused to be quenched. Although Judith had lost four children, we continued to stand on the promise of God which had been prophetically delivered to us: we would have a son! God is not a man that He should lie; His covenant word is forever settled in heaven. (Num. 23:19; Ps. 119:89.) That was the sliver of hope we hung onto throughout the whole ordeal.

I want you to realize that God always knows when you're at the end of your rope. He knows when you can't go any further. His word says that with every temptation, He will make a way of escape. (1 Cor. 10:13.) Whatever your situation, don't give up. Even if it has gone on for three weeks, or thirty-three years, all is not lost. God is working on your behalf. His word declares it. (Rom. 8:28.)

It was at this time, when we were literally at the end of our rope, that God began to release the keys to victory. We began to gain an understanding of spiritual warfare, of deliverance and the authority of the believer.

Learning to Release Faith

Judith became pregnant for the fifth time. We purposed to keep the news from everyone because of the voices of doubt and unbelief which kept speaking through our friends and relatives.

I took Judith to the doctor for tests, and he told us that if the baby somehow miraculously survived, it would be born some time around the middle of June. Toward the end of November, Judith's body came under the same physical attack as before. The baby's heartbeat stopped, and oxytocin was released into her system. (Oxytocin is the substance which is usually released after a miscarriage or the birth of an infant.)

After every previous miscarriage, oxytocin had been released into Judith's body, which caused it to begin to produce milk. So when this event occurred, we immediately knew that something was wrong, something tragic was taking place. Once again the powers of fear and unbelief began to attack our minds.

One afternoon as we were ministering on the east coast, a pastor felt impressed to pray for Judith. He didn't even know that she was pregnant, but he began to call forth the life and power of God into her body.

While we were praying for Judith, the power of God came into her, but it wasn't anything spectacular. Many times God will move in spectacular ways. I love the spectacular. *But one thing we must never forget is that the supernatural is not always spectacular.* Many times we look for the spectacular and overlook the supernatural.

So there was no bolt of lightning from heaven, no angelic choirs or clouds of glory. Nothing out of the ordinary happened. We simply left with an inner assurance that something had changed in our lives. Our faith in God's word had been released, which would have its effect.

God Is Faithful!

Shortly after we left the east coast, God began to give us more keys of understanding. He showed us several strategic things to do to bring about the completion of Judith's healing.

It wasn't long afterwards that the doctor picked up a heartbeat! We began to feel the baby move! Life had come back into the child!

From the first due date which the doctor had given Judith until the actual time the baby was born was a month and a half. She had carried that baby ten and a half months! The child had been dead in the womb for about six weeks or so. But our son was restored to life, brought to full term and safely delivered!

Stand Your Ground!

God is faithful. But one of the things I learned throughout the whole experience is how to war according to prophecy. If God has said something, then you can take that word and punch the devil with it!

If God has spoken to you through a word of prophecy, don't back away from it. That is one of the important lessons God has taught me in life. If He speaks, I will not budge from what He has said. No matter what the pressure is like.

Pressure is a killer of the will of God.

Regardless of how the circumstances of your life may appear, if God has given you a word of prophecy, stand your ground! Don't bow, don't bend, and don't break. Don't throw up your hands in despair. Begin to take the word of God and war with it. Let God's *rhema* come forth from your spirit. Say: "No devil, you won't have your way in my life. God's will shall come forth!"

Speak it out. Declare it. Boldly. Publicly. It doesn't matter if some people think you're strange. If you believe the word of God, you probably are already a bit strange to religious people. Just continue to stand on God's word, and you will see it fulfilled in your life.

9

Warring According to Prophecy

It came to pass after this also, that the children of Moab, and the children of Ammon, and with them other beside the Ammonites, came against Jehoshaphat to battle....

Then upon Jahaziel..., a Levite of the sons of Asaph, came the Spirit of the Lord in the midst of the congregation;

And he said, Hearken ye, all Judah, and ye inhabitants of Jerusalem, and thou king Jehoshaphat, thus saith the Lord unto you, Be not afraid nor dismayed by reason of this great multitude; for the battle is not yours, but God's.

To morrow go ye down against them: behold, they come up by the cliff of Ziz; and ye shall find them at the end of the brook, before the wilderness of Jeruel.

Ye shall not need to fight in this battle: set yourselves, stand ye still, and see the salvation of the Lord with you, O Judah and Jerusalem: fear not, nor be dismayed; to morrow go out against them: for the Lord will be with you.

And Jehoshaphat bowed his head with his face to the ground: and all Judah and the inhabitants of Jerusalem fell before the Lord, worshipping the Lord.

And the Levites, of the children of the Hohathites, and of the children of the Korhites, stood up to praise the Lord God of Israel with a loud voice on high.

And they rose early in the morning, and went forth into the wilderness of Tekoa: and as they went

> forth, Jehoshaphat stood and said, Hear me, O Judah, and ye inhabitants of Jerusalem; Believe in the Lord your God, so shall ye be established; believe his prophets, so shall ye prosper....

> And when they began to sing and to praise, the Lord set ambushments against the children of Ammon, Moab, and mount Seir, which were come against Judah; and they were smitten.

> **2 Chronicles 20:1,14-20,22**

In this passage we see that King Jehoshaphat knew how to war according to prophecy. When the prophetic word came forth to him, he knew he was to obey that word unreservedly. He began to operate his faith to do exactly what God had spoken. He knew that the blessings of God would come upon him and that his enemies would be defeated because of his obedience to God's revealed word.

To the natural mind Jehoshaphat's instructions to the people were foolish. *Any military strategists will inform you that songs won't stop arrows, swords or spears.* **But God hath chosen the foolish things of the world to confound the wise; and God hath chosen the weak things of the world to confound the things which are mighty** (1 Cor. 1:27).

Now I would like for you to notice very carefully that these Israelites were skilled in warfare. They knew how to fight. They had been trained in waging war. But that wasn't God's intention for this battle. God's strategy was for them to obey the word of the prophecy. His plan was for them to release their faith in His *rhema*.

We must inquire of the Lord on our way to every battlefield of life. Just because yesterday's strategies worked for yesterday's battle does not mean that they are God's plans for today. Too many times we rely on past battle plans instead of paying the price in prayer to receive heaven's strategy for today.

Picture these warriors on the battlefield. They have their weapons at hand. They are well trained in battle tactics. They are eagerly waiting for the approach of the enemy. The closer he comes, the stronger their natural instinct to draw their swords and fight!

I imagine these veteran warriors were somewhat like the gunslingers of the Old West, just watching for the enemy to "make his move" so they could "draw down" on him! Their weapons were ready, the enemy was advancing toward them, the natural strategies of war had been burned into their minds. They were all set to charge. But there was just one problem: *Heaven's strategies and earth's strategies are very seldom the same.* Instead of attacking, the warriors were ordered by the king to stand still while "the choir" began to sing and praise the Lord! The Lord "set ambushments" against the enemy and he was defeated and destroyed.

Many people fail in spiritual warfare for one important reason: instead of trusting in the Lord and obeying His word, they lean on their own understanding. Just about the time the Lord is ready to come through and perform a miracle on their behalf, they decide to draw their swords and wage war in the flesh. But not Jehoshaphat! He and his people stood still, as the Lord had commanded. They trusted in the Lord and obeyed His word, and the victory was accomplished.

What was the secret of their success? The secret was trusting the Lord and obeying His word.

Warring Through to Victory!

Now Elisha was fallen sick of his sickness whereof he died. And Joash the king of Israel came down unto him, and wept over his face, and said, O my father, my father, the chariot of Israel, and the horsemen thereof.

And Elisha said unto him, Take bow and arrows. And he took unto him bow and arrows.

And he said to the king of Israel, Put thine hand upon the bow. And he put his hand upon it: and Elisha put his hands upon the king's hands.

And he said, Open the window eastward. And he opened it. Then Elisha said, Shoot. And he shot. And he said, The arrow of the Lord's deliverance, and the arrow of deliverance from Syria: for thou shalt smite the Syrians in Aphek, till thou have consumed them.

2 Kings 13:14-17

So the prophetic word came to the king of Israel. He was given the opportunity to war according to prophecy.

And he said, Take the arrows. And he took them. And he said unto the king of Israel, Smite upon the ground. And he smote thrice, and stayed.

And the man of God was wroth with him, and said, Thou shouldest have smitten five or six times; then hadst thou smitten Syria till thou hadst consumed it: whereas now thou shalt smite Syria but thrice.

2 Kings 13:18,19

The king began to war with prophecy, but he didn't war in enough power, until the compete breakthrough.

When you step out to war for those prophecies to come to pass, you must not give up after only three attempts. You must learn to "endure hardness, as a good soldier of Jesus Christ"! (2 Tim. 2:3.) Keep hitting the ground! No matter how hard the ground, or how tired your hand becomes, keep fighting until every enemy in your life is defeated.

You cannot war for three days and give up. Keep warring until every enemy has become your footstool. Don't let discouragement defeat you on the brink of your greatest breakthrough!

If you want to see prophecies fulfilled in your life, by faith begin to stir them up inside of you. Keep them alive. Pray them out in the Spirit in other tongues with groanings, weepings and travail. Declare and decree them. This is how to war according to prophecy. Take every available weapon and bombard heaven and hell until the prophecy is manifested in your life. Don't give up. Don't quit prematurely on the edge of victory.

A wise man once said, *"Upon the plains of hesitation, bleach the bones of countless thousands, who upon the threshold of victory sat down to wait, and while they waited, wasted and died."*

Arise! Stir up those prophetic words! Engage in the fight of faith! Your destiny in God awaits!